WITHDRAWN

HAZEN MEMORIAL LIBRARY
3 KEADY WAY
SHIRLEY, MA 01464
978-425-2620

1/9/07 Lookout Pts. $31.59

MARTIN LUTHER KING JR.

Published by Creative Education
123 South Broad Street
Mankato, Minnesota 56001
Creative Education is an imprint of The Creative Company.

DESIGN AND PRODUCTION **EVANSDAY DESIGN**

PHOTOGRAPHS BY Corbis (Bettmann, Flip Schulke),
Getty Images (William Lovelace, Paul Schutzer//Time Life Pictures)

Nobel Peace Prize speech by Martin Luther King Jr. © The Nobel
Foundation, 1964. Reprinted by permission. / "What Is Your Life's
Blueprint?" by Martin Luther King Jr. Copyright 1967 Martin Luther
King Jr., copyright renewed 1991 Coretta Scott King. Reprinted by
arrangement with the Estate of Martin Luther King Jr., c/o Writers
House as agent for the proprietor New York, NY.

Copyright © 2006 Creative Education
International copyright reserved in all countries.
No part of this book may be reproduced in any form
without written permission from the publisher.
Printed in the United States of America.

LIBRARY OF CONGRESS CATALOGING-IN-PUBLICATION DATA
Fandel, Jennifer.
Martin Luther King, Jr. / by Jennifer Fandel.
p. cm. – (Genius)
Summary: Describes the life and legacy of Martin Luther King, Jr.,
twentieth-century civil rights leader.
ISBN 1-58341-329-4
1. King, Martin Luther, Jr., 1929–1968–Juvenile literature. 2. African
Americans–Biography–Juvenile literature. 3. Civil rights workers–United
States–Biography–Juvenile literature. 4. Baptists–United States–Clergy–
Biography–Juvenile literature. 5. African Americans–Civil rights–His-
tory–20th century–Juvenile literature. 6. Civil rights movements–United
States–History–20th century–Juvenile literature.
[1. King, Martin Luther, Jr., 1929–1968. 2. Civil rights workers. 3. Clergy.
4. African Americans–Biography. 5. Civil rights movements–History.]
I. Title. II. Genius (Mankato, Minn.)

E185.97.K5F36 2004
323'.092–dc22   2003065226

First edition

9 8 7 6 5 4 3 2 1

[M A R T I N   L U T H E R   K I N G   J R .]

GENiUS

Jennifer Fandel

xcellencies, ladies and gentlemen: I accept the Nobel on Negroes of the United States are engaged in a tice. I accept this award on behalf of a civil rights ajestic scorn for risk and danger to establish a reign ly yesterday in Birmingham, Alabama, our children ses, snarling dogs, and even death. I am mindful that le seeking to secure the right to vote were brutalized inding poverty afflicts my people and chains them I must ask why this prize is awarded to a movement uggle, and to a movement which has not yet won the Nobel Prize. After contemplation, I conclude that t, is a profound recognition that nonviolence is the of our time: the need for man to overcome oppression ession. civilization and violence are antithetical people of India, have demonstrated that nonviolence ich makes for social transformation. Sooner or later ay to live together in peace, and thereby transform therhood. If this is to be achieved, man must evolve , aggression, and retaliation. The foundation of such in Montgomery, Alabama, to Oslo bears witness t Negroes are traveling to find a new sense of dignity f progress and hope. It has led to a new civil rights thened into a superhighway of justice as Negro an vercome their common problems. I accept this award acious faith in the future of mankind. I refuse t es of history. I refuse to accept the idea that the capable of reaching up for the eternal "ought-ness"

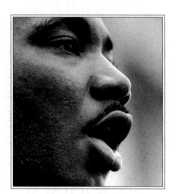

HIS VOICE SEIZED THE CROWD.

RICH, LYRICAL, AND IMPASSIONED, HIS VOICE REACHED HARD-

ENED HEARTS AND WEARY SOULS, AWAKENING A DESIRE FOR WHAT

MANY HAD LEARNED TO LIVE WITHOUT: FREEDOM. SPEAKING THAT

SIMPLE WORD, MARTIN LUTHER KING JR. IGNITED THE DREAMS OF

AFRICAN AMERICANS THROUGHOUT THE SOUTH, AND HE TOUCHED

PEOPLE—OF ALL COLORS, CREEDS, AND BACKGROUNDS—THROUGHOUT

THE UNITED STATES AND AROUND THE GLOBE. LEADING THE CIVIL

RIGHTS MOVEMENT IN THE 1950S AND '60S, HE INSPIRED MORE

THAN PEACEFUL PROTESTS AND MARCHES FOR EQUALITY. HE IN-

SPIRED MORE THAN THE JUSTICE OF NEW LAWS. THROUGH HIS

WORDS AND ACTIONS, HE LEFT A LEGACY OF HOPE AND A LASTING

VISION OF A WORLD ONE DAY UNITED BY THE POWER OF LOVE.

GENiUS

1 YOUNG, GIFTED, AND BLACK

MARTIN LUTHER KING JR. WAS BORN ON JANU-
ARY 15, 1929, INTO A LOVING, MIDDLE-CLASS FAM-
ILY. THE SON OF A BAPTIST MINISTER AND A FORMER
SCHOOLTEACHER, MARTIN, OR M. L., AS HIS FAM-
ILY CALLED HIM, GREW UP IN ATLANTA, GEORGIA,
WITH AN OLDER SISTER AND A YOUNGER BROTHER.

A segregationist sign in the South

Martin's father, Martin Luther King Sr., rose in life from difficult circum-
stances. The son of a Georgia sharecropper, he spent his childhood working
to help his family survive instead of attending school. Determined and
full of ambition, he left home at age 14 and traveled to Atlanta. While
working various jobs, he earned his high school diploma, graduated from
college, and began preaching in two country churches—all by the age of
20. He married Alberta Williams, a college-educated schoolteacher and
the daughter of the pastor of Atlanta's Ebenezer Baptist Church, of which
Martin Sr. became assistant pastor. Soon their children Christine, Martin
Jr., and Albert Daniel were born.

Throughout his childhood, Martin Jr. faced few of the hardships that
plagued blacks in the South. He was educated, well fed, and comfort-
ably sheltered in a two-story brick home, while many black children
lived in poverty, in ghettos or rickety housing, suffering the ache of
hunger, and working instead of going to school. But there was one
obstacle that education and income could not rise above: segregation.

Martin learned about segregation at the age of six through a white playmate. Until that time, Martin had not been exposed to the barriers of race, so he felt deeply hurt when his friend's father barred them from playing together. The reason he gave astounded Martin: Martin was black. When the father spoke, Martin heard the word "black" as more than a color. In the word were hidden connotations of dirtiness, difference, and being less than white. That day, Martin vowed that he would hate all white people; he would not accept being treated that way.

"I looked over toward Martin and Martin was very quietly sitting in the chair, and a tear ran down his cheek. It was a victory like none other, it was an affirmation of the movement …that millions of people in the South would have a chance to be involved in their own destiny."

REV. C. T. VIVIAN
SCLC ORGANIZER ON THE SIGNING
OF THE VOTING BILL

As a boy, Martin was curious and precocious. His parents enforced the importance of education, and he studied hard, reading voraciously and discussing his ideas. Riveted by words, he absorbed the preacher's sermons in church each Sunday, noticing how certain words could move the congregation to tears or shouts of praise. When a visiting preacher spoke one Sunday, Martin sat captivated by the man's eloquent vocabulary, his words as smooth as a prayer book in Martin's hands. After church, still in awe of the preacher's speech, Martin announced to his family, "Someday I'm going to have me some big words like that."

Throughout his grade school years, Martin's exposure to segregation grew. He became passionately resentful of the system that forced him to sit in the back of the bus, eat at separate lunch counters from whites, and attend different schools, but he didn't know how he could effect change. Then, a moment in high school foreshadowed his future role. Martin wrote a speech called "The Negro and the Constitution." Winning

In Atlanta, Georgia, parishioners frequently gathered outside the home church of Martin Luther King Jr. (pictured, bottom right) following Sunday services.

COLORED
WAITING ROOM
INTRASTATE PASSENGERS

"Martin said he would never himself resort to violence even in
self-defense, but he would not de-
mand that of others. That was a
religious commitment into which
one had to grow."

ANDREW YOUNG
SCLC ORGANIZER

the local oratorical contest with it, he traveled by public bus with his teacher to compete regionally. Even as a young teenager, Martin realized that the policy of segregation defied the laws penned in the United States Constitution. Not only was the message of his speech perceptive, his delivery was polished and passionate. He concluded his powerful speech, "And I with my brother of blackest hue possessing at last my rightful heritage and holding my head erect, may stand beside the Saxon—a Negro—and yet a man!"

Martin won the contest, but he was quickly reminded on his victory ride home that the road to freedom would be a long one. A white person boarded the bus and demanded Martin's seat. The teacher rose, but Martin, feeling defiant, stayed in his spot. The teacher encouraged him not to cause any trouble, and he moved, though reluctantly, standing for the long journey home. One day, he promised himself, one grand day, he would sit where he imagined his body to be—in the white area, in the front of the bus.

KING GRADUATES FROM HIGH SCHOOL AT THE AGE OF 15 AND ENROLLS AT MOREHOUSE COLLEGE, AN ALL-BLACK COLLEGE IN ATLANTA. *Timeline* **1944**

A black man exits the "Colored Waiting Room" in a Jackson,
Mississippi, bus terminal in 1961; King would fight to end this segregation.

2 ON THE PATH TO JUSTICE

GRADUATING FROM HIGH SCHOOL IN 1944, AT THE AGE OF 15, MARTIN ENROLLED FOR THE FALL SEMESTER AT HIS FATHER'S ALMA MATER, MORE-HOUSE COLLEGE, AN ALL-BLACK SCHOOL IN AT-LANTA. TO HELP PAY FOR COLLEGE AND SEE A BIT OF AMERICA, MARTIN TRAVELED NORTH TO CONNECTI-CUT FOR THE SUMMER TO WORK ON A TOBACCO FARM.

Workers on a tobacco farm

On Sundays, he served as the prayer leader for the 100 teenagers working on the farm. One Sunday, though, Martin and another young man went to church in town and were shocked to be the only blacks there. Cautious, but encouraged by the kind treatment they received, they ventured farther, eating at a nice restaurant in the city of Hartford. Martin enjoyed the freedom of integration that summer, but he once again felt the hard slap of segregation when, on the train ride home, blacks had to transfer to the Jim Crow car before entering the South.

Martin's first experience with integration and his education at Morehouse profoundly influenced him. The professors at More-house openly discussed the segregation problem and urged their students to work toward solutions. Martin joined the National Association for the Advancement of Colored People (NAACP) and the Intercollegiate Council, an organization that united all college students in Atlanta, black and white. In that organization, Martin

KING IS ORDAINED AS A BAPTIST MINISTER AND BECOMES THE ASSISTANT PASTOR OF EBENEZER BAPTIST CHURCH. *Timeline* 1947

met many forward-thinking whites who were dedicated to ending segregation. He began to see segregation not as a black problem, but as a human problem.

During this time, Martin's ideas about social action began to take shape. He discovered the writings of Henry David Thoreau and was greatly influenced by the essay "On Civil Disobedi-ence," in which Thoreau explained how disobeying unjust laws was an ethical method to bring about change. Later on in his education, Martin discovered the work of Mahatma Gandhi. Gandhi's strategy of nonviolent resistance, coupled with Thoreau's ideas, formed the basis of Martin's philosophy for overcoming white suppression.

While in college, Martin considered studying law to escape his father's expectation that he, too, would become a pastor. However, as he became more and more at-tracted to social justice work, he decided that he could best serve humanity through the church. The summer before his last year in college, at age 18, Martin was or-dained and named the assistant pastor of Ebenezer Baptist Church. During the de-livery of his first sermon, the congregation watched the boy they knew transform into a powerful man. He spoke with confidence and wisdom, his voice falling into the rhythms of preaching that he had listened to all his life. At the conclusion of his sermon, the congregation rose to their feet, showing their proud support with a standing ovation.

"King was out there in the streets. King, I think, was the catalyst for the great move-ments that were being made. King's suffer-ing was the catalyst. His being beaten, his being hosed, his being put in jail, all the suffering that he endured, in every case brought a legislative response."

HARRY McPHERSON
AIDE TO PRESIDENT LYNDON JOHNSON

Timeline **1948**   KING ENTERS GRADUATE SCHOOL AT CROZER THEOLOGICAL SEMINARY IN CHESTER, PENNSYLVANIA.

Blacks all across America seemed to be crying out for leadership in the middle of the 20th century; they would soon find their guide and voice in King.

"He was, in fact, a leader. He didn't
follow the crowd. He really did not
ask, 'Is this a popular position?'
Whatever positions he took, he took
those positions because he really
was convinced that the positions
he took were correct."

DOROTHY COTTON
SCLC STAFF MEMBER

But Martin did not believe in heeding God's call alone to minister; in fact, he had not yet heard His call. So, in 1948, after earning his bachelor's degree in sociology from Morehouse, Martin traveled north to Chester, Pennsylvania, for religious training at Crozer Theological Seminary. One of only six blacks in a class of 100, Martin graduated with top honors in May 1951 and was awarded a graduate fellowship. In early 1952, while working on his Ph.D. in theology at Boston University in Massachusetts, Martin met a beautiful, educated woman from Alabama named Coretta Scott. A gifted soprano studying at the New England Conservatory of Music, Coretta was working toward her dream of becoming a professional singer.

Martin was drawn to Coretta's intelligence and passion to end segregation in the South, and by the end of their first date, he hinted to Coretta that he would like her to be his wife. They married a year later, in the spring of 1953, and their four children—Yolanda, Martin Luther III, Dexter, and Bernice—were born in the following 10 years.

In 1954, Martin applied for a number of pastor positions—both in the North and the South. He and Coretta enjoyed the freedom they had in the North, unfettered by segregation. But when the pastorship of the Dexter Avenue Baptist Church in Montgomery, Alabama, was offered to him, Martin accepted. In Montgomery, Martin and Coretta saw a place to confront segregation and actively push for change.

KING ACCEPTS THE PASTOR POSITION AT DEXTER AVENUE BAPTIST CHURCH IN MONTGOMERY, ALABAMA. **Timeline 1954**

King married Coretta Scott, who was thrown into the spotlight with him;
in this photograph, the couple speaks to reporters in Montgomery, Alabama.

ANSWERING HIS CALL

ALABAMA, ONCE REFERRED TO AS THE "CRADLE OF THE CONFEDERACY" FOR ITS STRONG BELIEF IN STATES' RIGHTS, WAS AN OPPRESSIVE PLACE FOR BLACKS TO LIVE. ONLY ONE YEAR AFTER MARTIN BECAME A MONTGOMERY PASTOR, AN EVENT IN THE CITY CHANGED HISTORY AND SET MARTIN ON HIS PARTICULAR PATH TO JUSTICE. IN DECEMBER 1955, A BLACK WOMAN NAMED ROSA PARKS REFUSED TO GIVE UP HER BUS SEAT TO A WHITE MAN, SPARKING THE MONTGOMERY BUS BOYCOTT.

Civil rights pioneer Rosa Parks

On the first day of the boycott, buses roamed empty through the black neighborhoods while people walked, biked, or shared rides to get to work or school. To help rally continued support for the boycott, Martin spoke at a local church that first night. More than 5,000 people turned out to hear the 26-year-old pastor's inspirational preaching. He said, "If you will protest courageously, and yet with dignity and Christian love, future historians will say, 'There lived a great people—a black people—who injected new meaning and dignity into the veins of civilization.'" His words, filling the crowd with conviction, were met with resounding cheers.

Martin's success with the crowd convinced the other Montgomery pastors to elect him president of the Montgomery Improvement Association (MIA), a newly formed organization whose goal was to make Montgomery hospitable to blacks. Martin served as

KING IS ELECTED PRESIDENT OF THE MONTGOMERY IMPROVEMENT ASSOCIATION (MIA). *Timeline* **1955**

the black community's chief spokesperson throughout the boycott, arranging discussions between black leaders and Montgomery city officials.

In his new role, Martin and his family were subject to threats from white community members. The Ku Klux Klan set crosses ablaze on Martin's front lawn, and a bomb exploded near his house, drawing an angry group of blacks ready to seek revenge for their leader. Martin calmed the crowd, telling them, "We must meet hate with brotherly love."

As the threats grew, Martin worried for his family's safety. One night, after receiving an angry, late-night phone call, Martin sat at the kitchen table with his face in his hands, telling God of his fear and asking for guidance. There, in the darkened kitchen, Martin heard God's voice. Taking this as a sign of God's call, Martin felt more confident, believing that God would protect him in his mission.

In November 1956, the United States Supreme Court declared segregation on public buses unconstitutional, and a month later, Martin finally rode at the front of the bus. The struggle for desegregation dragged on for nearly a year, yet Martin saw how the boycott filled people throughout the South with hope. If the shackles of segregation could be loosened in Montgomery, Alabama, why couldn't millions of blacks throughout the South obtain their freedom, too?

Throughout 1957, Martin's reputation as a spokesperson for the civil rights movement continued to grow. He traveled more than half a million miles (805,000 km)

"When the president asked him, 'Dr. King, what if you fail?' he said, 'It will not be Martin King Jr. who failed. It will be America that failed.' He believed very firmly, reaffirmed his commitment in nonviolence as the most important weapon available to these people."

CORETTA SCOTT KING
ON HER HUSBAND'S WORK WITH
THE POOR PEOPLE'S CAMPAIGN

Timeline **1957**   KING IS ELECTED PRESIDENT OF THE SOUTHERN CHRISTIAN LEADERSHIP CONFERENCE (SCLC).

Rosa Parks sits at the front of a bus on December 21, 1956, in Montgomery, Alabama, after the Supreme Court ruled segregation on the city bus system illegal.

> *"That part of his genius was to understand that you could not have a movement simply based on promises of the future. That you had to deliver. And he had delivered on voting rights. He had delivered on public accommodations. He had delivered on the Montgomery bus boycott, and so many other things."*
>
> MICHAEL HARRINGTON
> POLITICAL ORGANIZER AND WRITER

around the world, delivering a total of 208 speeches. Martin also became the president of the Southern Christian Leadership Conference (SCLC), an organization of Southern ministers and other black leaders fighting segregation throughout the South. During the next three years, television networks, newspapers, and magazines clamored to follow Martin in his work, making his name and his calm, gentle face inseparable from the fight for freedom in the South.

There was, however, one drawback to Martin's success: He was rarely home to spend time with Coretta and their young family. Coretta dedicated herself to raising the children and managing the household alone so that Martin could fully devote himself to his work. In early 1960, Martin resigned from his pastor position in Montgomery and accepted the assistant pastor position at his father's church in Atlanta, providing him with more time for both the movement and his family.

In 1962 and 1963, Martin worked on one of his most successful campaigns: the struggle against segregation in Birmingham, Alabama. The Birmingham campaign revealed both the desperation of the movement and the fierce anger of many die-hard segregationists. The American public became outraged when they saw images of black schoolchildren and adults attacked by police dogs, beaten with clubs, and battered by the harsh spray of fire hoses. While some people had once dismissed segregation as a "Southern" problem, the graphic pictures on their television screens now convinced many Americans otherwise. This was clearly a "human" problem. People began to feel that Martin's cause was their cause, too.

KING DELIVERS HIS "I HAVE A DREAM" SPEECH IN WASHINGTON, D.C. *Timeline* **1963**

Racial tension and unrest in the South came to a head with the civil rights movement in the 1960s; in some places, violence against blacks intensified.

4 "I HAVE A DREAM"

THE MORNING OF AUGUST 28, 1963, SEEMED FULL OF PROMISE. THE SKIES ACROSS WASHINGTON, D.C., WERE VIBRANTLY BLUE AND CLOUDLESS, AND THE SUN'S EARLY HEAT HINTED AT A HOT DAY AHEAD. MOMENTUM HAD BEEN BUILDING THROUGHOUT THE UNITED STATES FOR AN END TO SEGREGATION IN THE SOUTH AND AN END TO DISCRIMINATION IN THE WORKFORCE NATIONWIDE.

President Lyndon B. Johnson shaking hands with King

Martin and the other organizers of the Washington March for Jobs and Freedom hoped that the march would help draw added attention to the civil rights bill pending at that time in Congress.

A steady stream of traffic tied up all roads leading into Washington. School buses and motor coaches, decorated with bright banners, pulled into the Washington Mall, carrying civil rights organizations, church groups, and individuals from every part of the nation. People poured into the capital on foot, by car, bicycle, and even roller skates. Some were attracted by King's presence, but even more were drawn by a feeling—a need—to be part of a movement that they believed in.

Surrounded by the other speakers and organizers of the march, Martin took his place at the podium. Dressed in a dark suit and tie, the clothes he wore to church each Sunday, Martin appeared both modest and professional. He scanned the enormous crowd stretched out before him, much farther than his eyes could see, and a hush fell over the crowd in anticipation of his words. And then Martin began to speak.

Believing that his speech should be more political than sermonic, Martin had pared down his verbal flourishes. But he was not entirely comfortable with this change and could hear from the crowd's reaction that his speech wasn't working its usual magic. Then, when he read the undulating line "We will not be satisfied until justice rolls down like waters and righteousness like a mighty stream," the crowd broke out into loud cheers and whoops of joy. Bolstered by their reaction, Martin raised his eyes away from his prepared speech and spoke instead from his heart, letting the words wash over him. He began with his now famous words, "I have a dream. . . ."

Martin's voice resonated with power and grace. "I have a dream," he said, "that my four little children will one day live in a nation where they will not be judged by the color of their skin but by the content of their character." And then, almost as if he were gathering his breath from the depths of his body, Martin rose onto the tips of his toes, gripped the podium, and cried out, "I have a dream today!"

As he continued to speak, Martin swayed his head back and forth in the steady rhythms of preaching, as if he were conjuring the words from a place deep inside himself. When he reached the end of his speech, his voice soared with these words:

> *"Though Martin Luther King has not personally committed himself to the international conflict, his own struggle is a clarion call to all who work for peace. . . . He is the first person in the Western world to have shown us that a struggle can be waged without violence."*
>
> GUNNAR JAHN
> MEMBER OF THE NORWEGIAN
> NOBEL COMMITTEE

> *"Because you did not seek fame, it has come to you. It must have been a person like you that Emerson had in mind when he said, 'See how the masses of men worry themselves into nameless graves when here and there a great, unselfish soul forgets himself into immortality.'"*
>
> REV. BENJAMIN MAYS
> ONE OF KING'S MOREHOUSE
> COLLEGE PROFESSORS

Timeline **1964**   KING IS AWARDED THE NOBEL PEACE PRIZE FOR HIS CAMPAIGN FOR INTEGRATION.

*Thousands gathered at Washington, D.C.'s Lincoln Memorial on August 28, 1963;
those in attendance heard King deliver his powerful "I Have a Dream" speech.*

"Though I had been opposed to going to Montgomery, I realize now
that it was an inevitable part of a
greater plan for our lives. Even in
1954 I felt that my husband was
being prepared—and I too—for a
special role about which we would
learn more later."

CORETTA SCOTT KING

When we allow freedom to ring, when we let it ring from every village and every hamlet, from every state and every city, we will be able to speed up that day when all of God's children, black men and white men, Jews and Gentiles, Protestants and Catholics, will be able to join hands and sing in the words of the old Negro spiritual, "Free at last, free at last. Thank God Almighty, we are free at last."

People cheered and wept, overcome with emotion, feeling the transforming power of Martin's words. In total, a quarter of a million people participated in what became known as the largest civil rights march in American history. Of the 250,000 marchers, 60,000 were white. This large number of white participants stunned the organizers and showed them that the issue had finally penetrated the national consciousness. Encouraged by this fact, Martin and the organizers were eager to attend a White House meeting immediately following the march. At the meeting, President John F. Kennedy stressed his deepening commitment to civil rights and promised to fully support the civil rights bill.

Leaving the White House and stepping out into that August evening, Martin felt victory in the humid summer air. He smiled, remembering all of the people who had stood united in spirit just hours ago—an image that seemed like a dream.

KING AND THE SCLC LEAD A VOTING CAMPAIGN IN THE SOUTH.   *Timeline* **1965**

*King's "I Have a Dream" speech, one of the most famous in American
history, became a landmark statement of the civil rights movement.*

TOWARD THE PROMISED LAND

DESPITE THE SPIRITED ASSEMBLY AT THE WASH-
INGTON MARCH, MANY IN THE UNITED STATES WERE
NOT READY TO SURRENDER THEIR BELIEFS IN SEGRE-
GATION. ONLY TWO WEEKS AFTER THE MARCH, FOUR
YOUNG BLACK GIRLS IN BIRMINGHAM, ALABAMA, WERE
KILLED WHEN DYNAMITE EXPLODED IN THEIR CHURCH.

King receiving the Nobel Peace Prize

Three months after the march, President Kennedy, the man who seemed determined to pass civil rights legislation, was assassinated. The new president, Lyndon Baines Johnson, rapidly took up the cause.

Victory for the movement came in 1964. In July of that year, President Johnson invited Martin to the White House to witness the signing of the Civil Rights Act of 1964, prohibiting segregation of public facilities and outlawing job discrimination. Months later, the world community bestowed on Martin its greatest honor: the Nobel Prize for Peace. At the age of 35, Martin was the youngest recipient of the prize ever.

But with the victories and honors came a greater sense of responsibility, and around this time, family and friends noticed a change in Martin. While he had always been driven by his work, Martin had also liked to indulge in good food, listen to music, and share jokes and stories. But he began to withdraw from life's pleasures, growing more serious in his religious beliefs. He still savored moments with his wife and children, but as he pressured himself to work harder, sensing that his time on Earth was running out, he saw less and less of them.

Martin's vision for a peaceful world began to take on new dimensions. In 1965, his campaign for black voting rights in the South ended in success with President Johnson's signing of the Voting Rights Act into law. This accomplished, Martin poured his energy into improving living conditions for the poor throughout the world. He spoke out against war, particularly the Vietnam War, and he and his colleagues in the SCLC organized the Poor People's Campaign, a march and camp-out to draw awareness to the poor in the United States. Some critics thought Martin was taking on causes too large for him to handle, but he continued his crusade despite the criticism.

On April 3, 1968, Martin arrived in Memphis, Tennessee, to speak at the Sanitation Workers' Strike rally. It was a stormy night, and Martin felt tired, so he convinced his friend Ralph Abernathy to go in his place. When Abernathy arrived at the rally, he sensed the crowd's disappointment and called Martin to come right away. When Martin arrived, the crowd was ecstatic, and the speech he delivered that night filled them with hope for their cause. Through the steady rain, Martin delivered these prophetic words:

"The dream of Dr. Martin Luther King Jr. has not died with him. Men who are white—men who are black—must and will now join together as never in the past to let all the forces of divisiveness know that America shall not be ruled by the bullet, but only by the ballot of free and of just men."

LYNDON BAINES JOHNSON
PRESIDENT OF THE UNITED
STATES FROM 1963 TO 1969

"My husband had always talked of his own readiness to give his life for a cause he believed in. He felt that giving himself completely would serve as a redemptive force in his inspiration to other people. This would mean that he would be resurrected in the lives of other people who dedicated themselves to a great cause."

CORETTA SCOTT KING

Timeline **1967** KING AND THE SCLC BEGIN WORK ON THE POOR PEOPLE'S CAMPAIGN.

On the eve of his murder in Memphis, Tennessee, King delivered his final speech, a strangely prophetic message that seemed to foretell his imminent death.

We've got some difficult days ahead. But it really doesn't matter with me now, because I've been to the mountaintop. And I don't mind. Like anybody, I would like to live a long life—longevity has its place. But I'm not concerned about that now. I just want to do God's will. And He's allowed me to go up to the mountain. And I've looked over, and I've seen the promised land. I may not get there with you. But I want you to know tonight, that we, as a people, will get to the promised land. And I'm happy tonight. I'm not worried about anything. I'm not fearing any man. Mine eyes have seen the glory of the coming of the Lord.

"There was a sense at Dr. King's funeral that we were at a moment in history that was unique. All those hundreds of thousands of people who came there had a sense of oneness that I've never quite experienced anywhere else again."

HARRY BELAFONTE
AMERICAN SINGER
AND ENTERTAINER

The next afternoon, Martin was killed by an assassin's bullet as he stood on the balcony of the Lorraine Motel in Memphis. The nation fell into mourning. The United States had lost not only a young leader; it had lost a visionary and a symbol of hope.

On the day of Martin's funeral in Atlanta, 100,000 people lined the streets of the funeral procession, and another 50,000 people gathered as they always did whenever his name was spoken: ready to march. Through the streets of Atlanta, they marched in their somber suits and dresses, behind Martin's grieving wife, children, and friends. Wondering if their tired feet would ever find rest, the marchers remembered his voice. It shattered their doubts, soothed their worries, and strengthened their resolve. They marched on, and continue to march today, his voice calling them to the promised land.

KING IS ASSASSINATED ON APRIL 4, IN MEMPHIS, TENNESSEE, AT THE AGE OF 39. *Timeline* **1968**

Five days after King's death, Coretta wore a black veil over her face at her husband's funeral in Atlanta, Georgia; enormous crowds gathered to say farewell.

IN HIS

WORDS

ON OCTOBER 26, 1967, SIX MONTHS BEFORE HE WAS ASSASSINATED,

DR. MARTIN LUTHER KING JR. GAVE THE FOLLOWING SPEECH TO A GROUP

OF STUDENTS AT BARRATT JUNIOR HIGH SCHOOL IN PHILADELPHIA.

IN IT, DR. KING NOT ONLY EMPHASIZED THE INDIVIDUAL WORTH

AND SIGNIFICANCE OF EACH STUDENT, BUT ALSO CHALLENGED THEM

TO DO AND BE THEIR BEST NO MATTER WHERE LIFE LED THEM.

WHAT IS YOUR LIFE'S BLUEPRINT? *I want to ask*

you a question, and that is: What is your life's Blueprint?

Whenever a building is constructed, you usually have

an architect who draws a blueprint, and that blueprint

serves as the pattern, as the guide, and a building is not

well-erected without a good, solid blueprint.

Now each of you is in the process of building the structure of your lives, and the question is whether you have a proper, a solid, and a sound blueprint.

I want to suggest some of the things that should begin your life's blueprint. Number one, in your life's blueprint, should be a deep belief in your own dignity, your worth, and your own somebodiness. Don't allow anybody to make you feel that you're nobody. Always feel that you count. Always feel that you have worth, and always feel that your life has ultimate significance.

Secondly, in your life's blueprint you must have as the basic principle the determination to achieve excellence in your various fields of endeavor. You're going to be deciding as the days, as the years unfold what you will do in life—what your life's work will be. Set out to do it well.

And I say to you, my young friends, doors are opening to you—doors of opportunities that were not open to your mothers and your fathers—and the great challenge facing you is to be ready to face these doors as they open.

Ralph Waldo Emerson, the great essayist, said in a lecture in 1871, "If a man can write a better book or preach a better sermon or make a better mousetrap than his neighbor, even if he builds his house in the woods, the world will make a beaten path to his door."

This hasn't always been true—but it will become increasingly true, and so I would urge you to study hard, to burn the midnight oil; I would say to you, don't drop out of school. I understand all the sociological reasons, but I urge you that in spite of your economic plight, in spite of the situation that you're forced to live in—stay in school.

And when you discover what you will be in your life, set out to do it as if God Almighty called you at this particular moment in history to do it. Don't just set out to do a good job. Set out to do such a good job that the living, the dead, or the unborn couldn't do it any better.

If it falls your lot to be a street sweeper, sweep streets like Michelangelo painted pictures, sweep streets like Beethoven composed music, sweep streets like Leontyne Price sings before the Metropolitan Opera. Sweep streets like Shakespeare wrote poetry. Sweep streets so well that all the hosts of heaven and earth will have to pause and say: Here lived a great street sweeper who swept his job well. If you can't be a pine at the top of the hill, be a shrub in the valley. Be the best little shrub on the side of the hill.

Be a bush if you can't be a tree. If you can't be a highway, just be a trail. If you can't be a sun, be a star. For it isn't by size that you win or fail. Be the best of whatever you are.

———————————

WHEN DR. KING ACCEPTED THE 1964 NOBEL PEACE PRIZE, HE DID SO ON BEHALF OF THE MILLIONS OF BLACK AMERICANS WHO WERE STRUGGLING TO CARRY THE CIVIL RIGHTS MOVEMENT FORWARD IN COMMUNITIES ACROSS THE UNITED STATES. DR. KING'S MESSAGE IS ONE OF JUSTICE, BROTHERHOOD, AND LOVE, ACHIEVED THROUGH HIS EVER-PRESENT THEME OF OVERCOMING OPPRESSION WITH NONVIOLENCE. THE FOLLOWING SPEECH IS A POIGNANT SUMMARY OF DR. KING'S FIRMLY HELD BELIEFS AND HOPES FOR THE FUTURE OF ALL MANKIND.

ADDRESS DELIVERED IN ACCEPTANCE OF NOBEL PEACE PRIZE

DECEMBER 10, 1964, OSLO, NORWAY

Your Majesty, Your Royal Highness, Mr. President, excellencies, ladies and gentlemen: I accept the Nobel Prize for Peace at a moment when twenty-two million Negroes of the United States are engaged in a creative battle to end the long night of racial injustice. I accept this award on behalf of a civil rights movement which is moving with determination and a majestic scorn for risk and danger to establish a reign of freedom and a rule of justice.

I am mindful that only yesterday in Birmingham, Alabama, our children, crying out for brotherhood, were answered with fire hoses, snarling dogs, and even death. I am mindful that only yesterday in Philadelphia, Mississippi, young people seeking to secure the right to vote were brutalized and murdered. I am mindful that debilitating and grinding poverty afflicts my people and chains them to the lowest rung of the economic ladder.

Therefore, I must ask why this prize is awarded to a movement which is beleaguered and committed to unrelenting struggle, and to a movement which has not yet won the very peace and brotherhood which is the essence of the Nobel Prize. After contemplation, I conclude that this award, which I receive on behalf of that movement, is a profound recognition that nonviolence is the answer to the crucial political and moral questions of our time: the need for man to overcome oppression and violence without resorting to violence and oppression.

Civilization and violence are antithetical concepts. Negroes of the United States, following the people of India, have demonstrated that nonviolence is not sterile passivity, but a powerful moral force which makes for social transformation. Sooner or later, all the peoples of the world will have to discover a way to live together in peace, and thereby transform this pending cosmic elegy into a creative psalm of brotherhood. If this is to be achieved, man must evolve for all human conflict a method which rejects revenge, aggression, and retaliation. The foundation of such a method is love.

The torturous road which has led from Montgomery, Alabama, to Oslo bears witness to this truth, and this is a road over which millions of Negroes are traveling to find a new sense of dignity. This same road has opened for all Americans a new era of progress and hope. It has led to a new civil rights bill, and it will, I am convinced, be widened and lengthened into a superhighway of justice as Negro and white men in increasing numbers create alliances to overcome their common problems.

I accept this award today with an abiding faith in America and an audacious faith in the future of mankind. I refuse to accept despair as the final response to the ambiguities of history.

I refuse to accept the idea that the "is-ness" of man's present nature makes him morally incapable of reaching up for the eternal "ought-ness" that forever confronts him.

I refuse to accept the idea that man is mere flotsam and jetsam in the river of life, unable to influence the unfolding events which surround him.

I refuse to accept the view that mankind is so tragically bound to the starless midnight of racism and war that the bright daybreak of peace and brotherhood can never become a reality.

I refuse to accept the cynical notion that nation after nation must spiral down a militaristic stairway into the hell of nuclear annihilation.

I believe that unarmed truth and unconditional love will have the final word in reality. This is why right, temporarily defeated, is stronger than evil triumphant.

I believe that even amid today's mortar bursts and whining bullets, there is still hope for a brighter tomorrow.

I believe that wounded justice, lying prostrate on the blood-flowing streets of our nations, can be lifted from this dust of shame to reign supreme among the children of men.

I have the audacity to believe that peoples everywhere can have three meals a day for their bodies, education and culture for their minds, and dignity, equality, and freedom for their spirits.

I believe that what self-centered men have torn down, men other-centered can build up.

I still believe that one day mankind will bow before the altars of God and be crowned triumphant over war and bloodshed and nonviolent redemptive goodwill proclaimed the rule of the land. And the lion and the lamb shall lie down together, and every man shall sit under his own vine and fig tree, and none shall be afraid.

I still believe that we shall overcome.

This faith can give us courage to face the uncertainties of the future. It will give our tired feet new strength as we continue our forward stride toward the city of freedom. When our days become dreary with low-hovering clouds and our nights become darker than a thousand midnights, we will know that we are living in the creative turmoil of a genuine civilization struggling to be born.

Today I come to Oslo as a trustee, inspired and with renewed dedication to humanity. I accept this prize on behalf of all men who love peace and brotherhood. I say I come as a trustee, for in the depths of my heart I am aware that this prize is much more than an honor to me personally. Every time I take a flight I am always mindful of the many people who make a successful journey possible, the known pilots and the unknown ground crew. You honor the dedicated pilots of our struggle, who have sat at the controls as the freedom movement soared into orbit. You honor, once again, Chief Lutuli of South Africa, whose struggles with and for his people are still met with the most brutal expression of man's inhumanity to man. You honor the ground crew, without whose labor and sacrifice the jet flights to freedom could never have left the earth. Most of these people will never make the headlines, and their names will never appear in Who's Who. *Yet, when years have rolled past and when the blazing light of truth is focused on this marvelous age in which we live, men and women will know and children will be taught that we have a finer land, a better people, a more noble civilization because these humble children of God were willing to suffer for righteousness' sake.*

I think Alfred Nobel would know what I mean when I say I accept this award in the spirit of a curator of some precious heirloom which he holds in trust for its true owners: all those to whom truth is beauty, and beauty, truth, and in whose eyes the beauty of genuine brotherhood and peace is more precious than diamonds or silver or gold. Thank you.

BAPTIST A member of a religion characterized by the belief in God and Jesus, as well as the authority of the Bible. Baptists often receive their baptism as teenagers or adults to mark their chosen faith in God.

BOYCOTT The act of refusing to buy items, use services, or deal with certain people as a way to show disapproval or force changes to happen.

CIVIL RIGHTS MOVEMENT An organized effort in the 1950s and '60s for African Americans to obtain equal treatment, equal opportunities, and equal protection under the law, especially pertaining to voting, employment, and the use of public facilities.

CONFEDERACY A group of 11 southern states, including Alabama, Arkansas, Florida, Georgia, Louisiana, Mississippi, North Carolina, South Carolina, Tennessee, Texas, and Virginia, that seceded from the United States during the Civil War (1861–65).

HENRY DAVID THOREAU An American writer living in the early 1800s whose essay "On Civil Disobedience" addressed his refusal to pay taxes as a way to protest the Spanish-American War.

JIM CROW A name given to Southern laws that enforced segregation and unequal treatment of blacks. The name referred to a character in an early African-American minstrel show.

JOHN F. KENNEDY The 35th president of the United States. A Democrat and supporter of civil rights, Kennedy took office in 1961 and was assassinated on November 22, 1963.

KU KLUX KLAN (KKK) A secret society of whites that used methods of terror, such as burning crosses and hanging and maiming blacks, to maintain white supremacy in the South.

MOHANDAS GANDHI   The leader of India who developed the idea of peaceful resistance to gain independence from British rule. Assassinated in 1948, Gandhi was often referred to as Mahatma, a word meaning "great soul."

NATIONAL ASSOCIATION FOR THE ADVANCEMENT OF COLORED PEOPLE (NAACP)   An organization formed in 1909 to abolish discrimination and promote equality for blacks. The organization continues to be active in the 21st century.

SEGREGATION   The practice of keeping people separated based on their skin color. Blacks had to sit in different areas than whites, attend different schools, and use separate restrooms and drinking fountains.

SOUTHERN CHRISTIAN LEADERSHIP CONFERENCE (SCLC)   An organization of Southern pastors and their supporters who planned actions such as sit-ins, protests, and boycotts to help abolish segregation in the South.

STATES' RIGHTS   The belief that individual states should have the power to make their own laws instead of following the laws of the United States government.

THEOLOGY   The formal study of religion, focusing on the study of God and the relationship among God, humans, and the world.

VIETNAM WAR   A prolonged war, lasting from 1954 to 1975, involving communist and anticommunist armies in Vietnam, as well as their supporters. Large-scale United States involvement began in the mid-1960s and lasted until 1973.

WITHDRAWN

HAZEN MEMORIAL LIBRARY
3 KEADY WAY
SHIRLEY, MA 01464
978-425-2620